KT-555-848

WILD about

BOATS

By Steve Parker
Technical Consultant: Keith Faulkner
of Jane's Defence Weekly

Stats and Facts • Top makes • Top models • Top speeds

WILD about
BOATS

First published in Great Britain in 2003 by ***ticktock*** Media Ltd.,
Unit 2, Orchard Business Centre, North Farm Road, Tunbridge Wells, Kent, TN2 3XF
We would like to thank: Tim Bones, Keith Faulkner of *Janes* and Elizabeth Wiggans
Picture credits: Alamy: P6-7 all, P21t, P25t. Beken of Cowes: P12c, P18-19c. British Antarctic Survey: P14-15 all. Corbis: P8-9c, P16-17 all, P19t, P20c. Hawkes Ocean Technologies: P9t. John Clark Photography: P4-5c. RNLI: P28-29. Stena: P24c. World of Residensea: P26-27 all. Yamaha: P23t.
ISBN 1 86007 363 8 HB
ISBN 1 86007 369 7 PB
Printed in China.
A CIP catalogue record for this book is available from the British Library.

CONTENTS

CALIFORNIA QUAKE DRAG BOAT

The fastest racing boats on the water are drag boats. These single seater craft surge like rockets at breathtaking speeds over the waves, often spending more time above the surface than on it. This incredible machine has reached speeds of about 230 mph!

DID YOU KNOW?

Drag boat racing attracts crowds of up to one million people.

The Californian Quake's 5,000 **hp** engine let it become the first boat to race to ¼ mile in under 5 seconds - a world record!

Bottled air is supplied to the driver's helmet. This is so in the event of a crash, he can carry on breathing whilst waiting for divers to rescue him.

STATS AND FACTS

LAUNCHED: *1999*

ORIGIN: *USA*

ENGINES: *500 cubic inch nitromethane engine generating 5,000 hp*

LENGTH: *7.62 metres*

WIDTH: *3.72 metres*

MAX SPEED: *198 knots (230 mph)*

MAX WEIGHT: *4.75 tonnes*

LOAD: *1 pilot*

FUEL CAPACITY: *20 litres*

COST: *£60,000*

The most important part of the boat is the safety capsule. Complete with **rollcage**, it breaks free from the boat in the event of a high speed crash.

JUNE LEE CHINESE JUNK

The junk is one of the oldest boat designs. The first types were sailing over 2,000 years ago. Later they were used for trading goods all around East Asia. Junks still carry goods today - from rice and timber to computers and cars!

The **sails** are made of woven **linen** or similar fibres. They are held together by a frame made from long poles of bamboo or wood.

DID YOU KNOW?

Today the word 'junk' means old rubbish. But long ago it was an important word in Chinese – 'chu-ong', meaning 'boat'.

The **hull** is divided into separate compartments by cross-walls called **bulkheads**. If water leaks into one, it cannot spread to the others, so the ship stays afloat.

STATS AND FACTS

LAUNCHED: *1962*

ORIGIN: *Thailand*

ENGINES: *One generating 380 hp*

LENGTH: *33 metres*

WIDTH: *8.5 metres*

MAX SPEED: *8 knots (9.2 mph)*

MAX WEIGHT: *5.4 tonnes*

LOAD: *10 person crew plus 18 passengers*

FUEL CAPACITY: *10,000 litres*

COST: *£1.25 million*

Many junks now have **engines**, for when the wind drops. They also have **satellite navigation** to help them find their way.

DEEP FLIGHT SUBMERSIBLE

DID YOU KNOW?

A trip in a submersible down to the sunken wreck of the giant liner Titanic costs about £25,000.

Submersibles are like miniature submarines. They are used for deep sea exploration. Deep Flight is a tiny one-person submersible that does not use **buoyancy** (air/water) tanks. Instead it has short wings that let it 'fly' through the water.

The main body is made of a light material strong enough to resist the high pressure of water outside the submersible.

Deep Flight has a pair of stubby wings. Unlike the wings on a plane, though, these wings pull Deep Flight down through the water instead of up off the ground.

STATS AND FACTS

LAUNCHED: *1996*

ORIGIN: *USA*

ENGINES: *Two electric motors powered by ten 12 volt lead acid batteries, generating 5 hp each*

LENGTH: *4 metres*

WIDTH: *2.4 metres*

MAX SPEED: *12 knots (13.8 mph)*

MAX WEIGHT: *1.3 tonnes*

ASCENT RATE: *198 metres per minute*

DESCENT RATE: *150 metres per minute*

MAXIMUM DEPTH: *1,000 metres*

LOAD: *1 pilot*

COST: *£1 million*

Deep Flight is equipped with up to four cameras and six lights. These are needed because the deep sea is totally dark.

ENDEAVOUR SHIP-RIGGED BARK

Today we can travel around the world in just two days. Back in 1768, however, it took Captain James Cook almost three years to make the journey in his ship Endeavour. In 1988 work began on a replica of this incredible ship. In 1994, it sailed around the world to replicate the voyage of the original craft.

DID YOU KNOW?

The original Endeavour began life as a coal-carrier, and ended up as a French whaling ship.

While ordinary crew slept in hammocks just 14 inches apart, the captain lived in luxury. The Great Cabin had sash windows, a dining table and stove, fine furniture, books and paintings.

STATS AND FACTS

LAUNCHED: *1993*

ORIGIN: *Australia*

ENGINES: *Two Caterpillar 3406B diesels generating 404 hp*

LENGTH: *42 metres*

WIDTH: *9.76 metres*

HEIGHT TO TOP MAST: *Over 30 metres*

MAX SPEED: *8 knots (9.2 mph)*

MAX WEIGHT: *397 tonnes*

LOAD: *6 permanent crew, 32 voyage crew and 8 other*

FUEL CAPACITY: *132,500 litres*

COST: *£6 million*

Endeavour has 12 **sails**. Each has a special name. The small triangular sail at the front is the **jib**, while the highest one on the middle mast is the main **topgallant**.

Extra planks on the hull slow down the damage caused by shipworms. These pests eat away wood at an incredible rate in tropical seas.

ILLBRUCK RACING YACHT

Every year the fastest yachts in the world get together for the *Round The World Yacht Race*. In 2002 it was won by illbrook. The eight yachts in the competition covered over 37,000 miles in total, taking almost nine months.

DID YOU KNOW?

The whole illbrook project - yacht, crew, back-up team, equipment, training, transport, supplies - cost nearly £16 million.

Round-the-world yachts battle giant waves, howling gales, collisions with icebergs and whales - and each other!

STATS AND FACTS

LAUNCHED: *2002*

ORIGIN: *Germany*

ENGINES: *n/a*

LENGTH: *19.5 metres*

WIDTH: *5.25 metres*

MAX SPEED: *36.75 knots (42 mph)*

MAX WEIGHT: *13.5 tonnes*

LOAD: *12 people*

COST: *£16 million*

Crews pull the cables for the **sails** using high-speed **winches** with long handles. The height of the tallest mast is 26 metres.

The illbruck's **satellite** communications centre contains telephone, email and video transmission facilities.

JAMES CLARK ROSS RESEARCH SHIP

One of the world's toughest ships, the James Clark Ross can smash its way through ice more than two metres thick. This vessel is actually a huge floating **laboratory**, used for exploring and carrying out scientific research in the freezing seas of Antarctica.

There are five main sets of laboratories and science rooms on board the James Clark Ross. More can be loaded onto the **deck**, in house-sized containers.

JAMES CLARK ROSS

The main **hull** is extra-strong. It is made of very thick **steel**, capable of pushing through ice and fending off bergs.

A compressed air system prevents ice from squeezing and cracking the hull by rolling the ship from side-to-side.

STATS AND FACTS

LAUNCHED: *1990*

ORIGIN: *Britain*

ENGINES: *Two x Wartsilla R32 (3.1 MW each) and two x Warsilla R22 (1.0 MW) engines delivering 8,500 hp*

LENGTH: *99 metres*

WIDTH: *18.85 metres*

MAX SPEED: *15.7 knots (18 mph)*

MAX WEIGHT: *5,732 tonnes*

LOAD: *12 officers, 15 crew, 1 doctor, 31 scientists (maximum)*

FUEL CAPACITY: *1,350 cubic metres*

COST: *£37.5 million*

James Clark Ross surveys the oceans, and measures depths and currents. It also acts as a floating weather station, and even searches for strange creatures of the deep.

LOS ANGELES FIREBOAT NO. 2

Although ships are surrounded by water, they sometimes catch fire. Their **engines** and fuel may go up in flames, or they might carry a cargo like oil, which can burn. Almost every big port has fireboats on hand to tackle emergencies. This vessel is one of the Los Angeles Fire Department's six fireboats.

DID YOU KNOW?

Firefighters wear breathing kits. This is because some kinds of poisonous smoke can kill in just a few seconds.

All parts of the fireboat are flameproof, in case there is an explosion of burning fuel nearby.

When dockside buildings catch fire, it is time to call in the fireboats. As well as fighting ordinary fires, they can tackle electrical blazes by spraying special foam rather than water.

STATS AND FACTS

LAUNCHED: *1925*

ORIGIN: *USA*

ENGINES: *Two 700 hp V-12 Cummins; three 380 hp 6 cylinder in-line Cummins; and two 525 hp V-12 2 cycle Detroits, plus six engines for pumps*

LENGTH: *30 metres*

WIDTH: *6 metres*

MAX SPEED: *17 knots (19.6 mph)*

MAX WEIGHT: *152 tonnes*

LOAD: *14 crew*

FUEL CAPACITY: *9,801 litres*

COST: *£135,550 (in 1925)*

Six powerful diesel-powered **pumps**, all with their own engines, suck in water from around the boat. Then they fire out powerful **jets** of water from water-guns. These can reach heights of more than 150 metres.

TMENT 2

NIMITZ-CLASS AIRCRAFT CARRIER

DID YOU KNOW?

Up to 20,000 meals are served every day to hungry sailors on board the Nimitz.

Nimitz-class aircraft carriers are the biggest warships ever built. Each of these US giants is a floating army, navy and air force. The Nimitz-class has a crew the size of a small town, which includes 3,360 ships crew and 2,500 air crew. This number doesn't even include the soldiers and pilots!

This supercarrier carries up to 85 planes and six helicopters, along with all their spares, tools, pilots and service crew. Jet fuel is stored in swimming-pool-sized tanks.

Supercarriers like the Nimitz-class aircraft carrier are equipped with the latest computers, **radar**, missiles and other equipment. It takes three years to re-fuel, re-equip and re-fit these monsters.

STATS AND FACTS

LAUNCHED: *1972*

ORIGIN: *USA*

ENGINES: *Two nuclear reactors powering 4 steam turbines producing 260,000 hp*

LENGTH: *333 metres*

WIDTH: *40.8 metres*

MAX SPEED: *More than 30 knots (35 mph)*

MAX WEIGHT: *Over 100,000 tonnes*

LOAD: *3,360 ships crew and 2,500 air crew*

COST: *£1.25 billion*

At 333 metres, the Nimitz-class carrier is nearly as long as the Empire State building is tall.

JAHRE VIKING OIL SUPERTANKER

The biggest ships in the world are the giant tankers which carry crude oil, or petroleum. Their precious cargo is used to make petrol and other fuels, but also plastics, paints and hundreds of other products. These huge tankers are bigger than islands and take 5 miles to slow down and stop!

DID YOU KNOW?

The holds in the Jahre Viking could hold St Paul's cathedral in London four times over.

Most of the ship is controlled by computer. The crew is usually about 35-40. They control the vessel and live in the comparatively small **stern** section of the ship.

Oil is pumped on board through pipes at the oil terminal or rig. It is pumped off again at a **refinery**.

STATS AND FACTS

LAUNCHED: *1979*

ORIGIN: *Japan*

ENGINES: *Four steam turbines (37,300 KW) generating 50,019 hp each*

LENGTH: *940 metres*

WIDTH: *141 metres*

MAX SPEED: *10 knots (11.5 mph)*

MAX WEIGHT: *647,955 tonnes fully laden, 564,763 tonnes, unladen*

CREW: *35 to 40 people*

LOAD: *4,240,865 barrels of oil*

FUEL CAPACITY: *20,000 litres*

COST: *£62.5 million*

The whole **deck** area can be as large as four soccer pitches. It can take several minutes to walk the length of the deck, so crew members sometimes use bicycles to get around!

POLARIS VIRAGE TX JETSKI

The jetski is a combination of motorcycle, water-ski and snow-mobile. These vehicles are used for surging across the waves at great speeds. You can also do stunts on them, and even turn somersaults! If you lose your grip and fall off the craft, the water-jet stops immediately.

DID YOU KNOW?

The jetski was developed in the late 1960s. The idea came from US motorcycle rider Clay Jacobson who was working for the Kawasaki Motorcycle Company at the time.

The engine turns a fan-like **impeller**. This sucks in water in through a large opening, and blasts it out the back as a fast, narrow **jet**.

Jetski riders perform amazing turns, jumps and loops. They can even dive competely under water! In calm conditions, with little wind or waves, riders can reach speeds of almost 52 knots (60 mph).

STATS AND FACTS

LAUNCHED: *2000*

ORIGIN: *USA*

ENGINE: *Polaris Marine 1200, producing 135 hp*

LENGTH: *3.06 metres*

WIDTH: *1.25 metres*

MAX SPEED: *52 knots (60 mph)*

MAX WEIGHT: *285 kg*

LOAD: *1 pilot*

FUEL CAPACITY: *77 litres*

COST: *Up to £8,000*

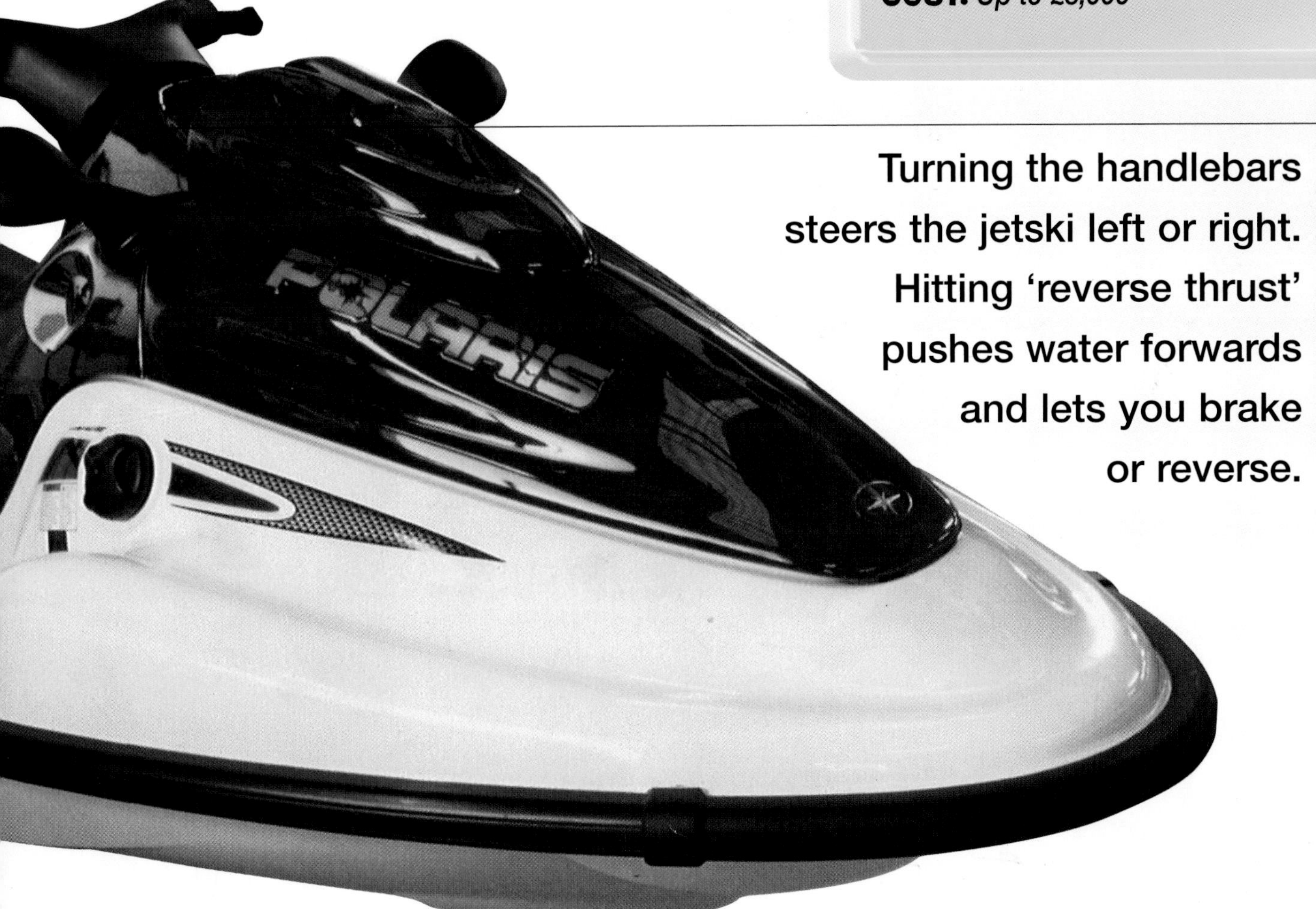

Turning the handlebars steers the jetski left or right. Hitting 'reverse thrust' pushes water forwards and lets you brake or reverse.

STENA DISCOVERY HSS FERRY

DID YOU KNOW?

Most car ferries are 'Ro-Ro' – roll (drive) on, and roll (drive) off. However, in the past cranes lifted each car on and off the boats.

Stena HSS ferries (High-speed Sea Service) are the largest fast car carriers in the world. They are **catamarans**, which means they have two **hulls** (main bodies) instead of one. The hulls cut through the waves giving a smoother and speedier ride.

The catamaran hulls are built mainly from the metal **aluminium**, This is because it is very light and does not rust in salt water.

Catamaran ferries operate across the world. This one serves the Caribbean and can hold more than 200 cars and 1,000 passengers. It has many lounge areas, bars and restaurants to keep passengers amused during the crossing.

STATS AND FACTS

LAUNCHED: *1997*

ORIGIN: *Finland*

ENGINES: *Two GE LM2500 gas turbines, generating 20,500 kW (27,490 hp) each, and two GE LM1600 gas turbines, producing 13,500 kW (18,103 hp) each*

LENGTH: *126.5 metres*

WIDTH: *40 metres*

MAX SPEED: *40 knots (46 mph)*

MAX WEIGHT: *1,500 tonnes*

LOAD: *1,500 passengers and 375 cars*

FUEL CAPACITY: *10,000 litres*

COST: *£65 million*

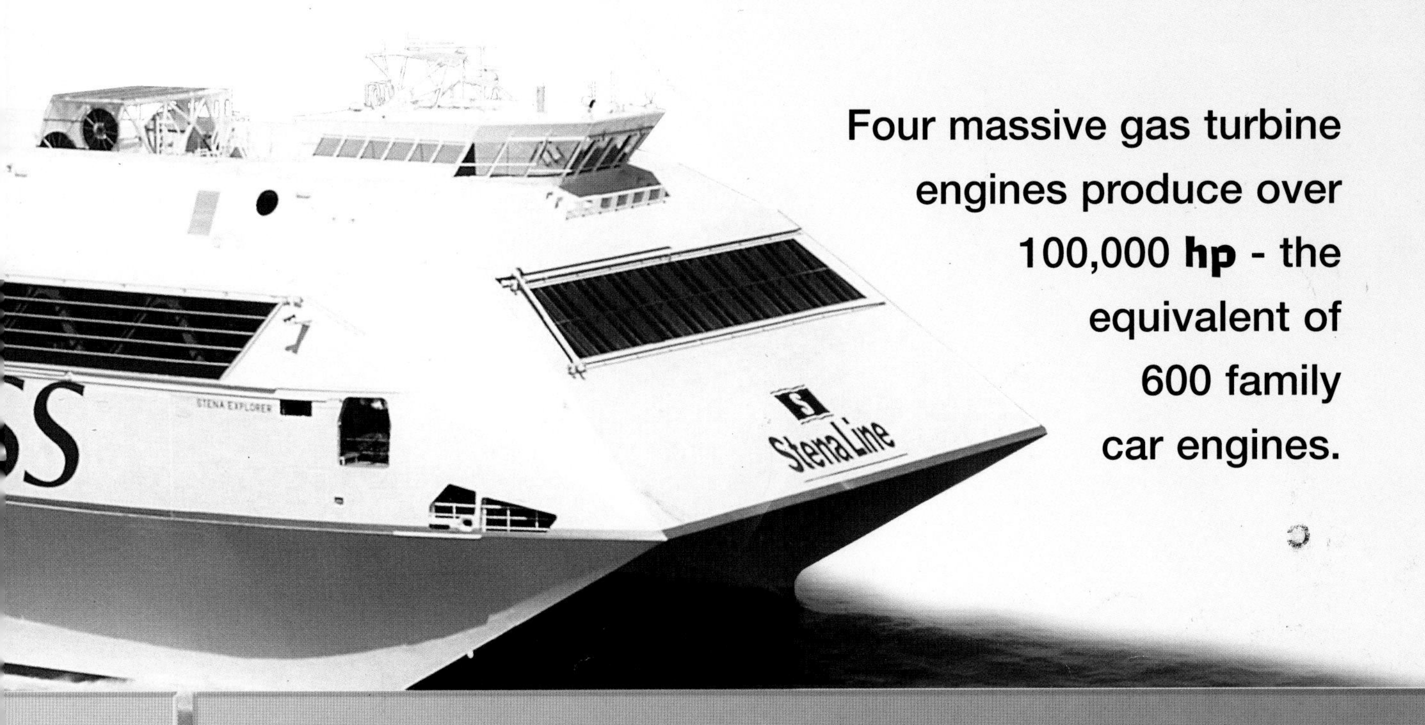

Four massive gas turbine engines produce over 100,000 **hp** - the equivalent of 600 family car engines.

THE WORLD LUXURY LINER

The World is a luxury **liner** with a difference - you live on it! For a vast price you can buy a set of rooms on board to make your permanent home. The ship travels to exciting world events, including the Rio de Janeiro carnival in Brazil and the Formula 1 Motor Race in Monaco.

DID YOU KNOW?

The cost of an apartment on The World ranges from £1.25 million to over £6 million.

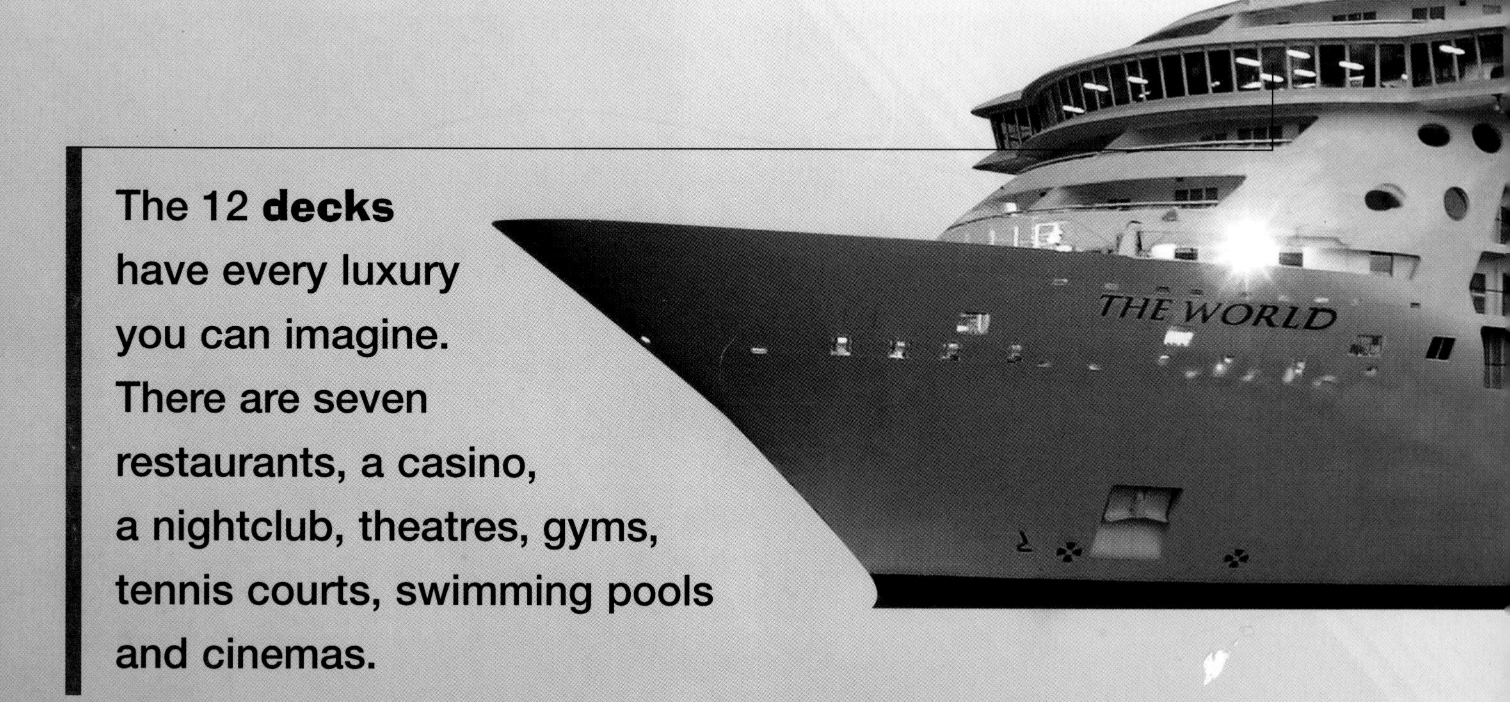

The 12 **decks** have every luxury you can imagine. There are seven restaurants, a casino, a nightclub, theatres, gyms, tennis courts, swimming pools and cinemas.

On The World, people are not passengers, but residents on a lifetime's holiday. There are 110 main residences, plus 88 extra apartments which can be rented out to guests.

STATS AND FACTS

LAUNCHED: *2001*

ORIGIN: *Norway*

ENGINES: *Two Wartsila 12 cylinder diesels, generating 5520 kW (7402 hp)*

LENGTH: *196.35 metres*

WIDTH: *29.8 metres*

MAX SPEED: *18.5 knots (21 mph)*

MAX WEIGHT: *43,524 tonnes*

LOAD: *Maximum of 976 residents, guests and crew*

FUEL CAPACITY: *1,150 cubic metres*

COST: *£164 million*

The **hull** of The World was built using giant pieces of **steel**, lifted into place using giant cranes.

TRENT-TYPE LIFEBOAT

DID YOU KNOW?

In the seas around Britain, lifeboats are called out between 15 and 20 times a day.

Every sailor has two terrible fears - shipwreck and drowning at sea. Brave lifeboat crews are always ready for rescue missions, and their boats must stay safe, even in the worst storms. The powerful Trent-type lifeboats are run by Britain's RNLI (Royal National Lifeboat Institution).

The hull of this lifeboat is made of various plastics, **carbon fibres** and other **composites**. Unlike metal these are very light but also very strong, and they never rust.

Special **radar** and radio equipment can track ships in distress. This technology uses the Marsat and Sarsat emergency **satellite navigation** systems.

STATS AND FACTS

LAUNCHED: *1994*

ORIGIN: *Britain*

ENGINES: *Two MAN diesels, 808 hp per engine, each about as powerful as a Formula 1 racing car engine*

LENGTH: *14.26 metres*

MAX SPEED: *25 knots (29 mph)*

MAX WEIGHT: *27.5 tonnes)*

LOAD: *6 crew plus 10 survivors*

FUEL CAPACITY: *4,100 litres*

COST: *£1.25 million*

The survivor's **cabin** has seats for 10 people. There are also heaters, dry clothes and a small **galley** serving hot drinks and snacks.

GLOSSARY

ALUMINIUM A lightweight, but strong, metal.

BARK Another name for a ship.

BRIDGE A ship's main control room from where it is steered. It is usually situated high up to provide good views in all directions.

BULKHEADS Dividing 'walls' that run across the inside of a ship, from side to side. They have doors for people to pass through.

BUOYANCY The upwards pushing force that water gives to objects, causing them to float if they are light enough.

CABIN A room or enclosed area on a ship or boat.

CARBON FIBRE A modern lightweight material used to make lots of types of vehicles.

CATAMARAN A boat or ship with two hulls, joined together by a wide deck or decks over the top.

COMPOSITE A material or substance which is made of a mixture of materials, such as plastics, metals and fibre-glass. Composites are usually very light and very strong.

DECKS The main floors or storeys of a ship, and especially the uppermost flat area where people walk about.

ENGINE The part of a vehicle where fuel is burned to create energy.

GALLEY The kitchen or dining area on a ship.

HULL The main part or body of a ship, which floats on the water.

HORSEPOWER (HP) The measure of an engine's power, originally based on the power of an engine compared to a horse.

IMPELLER A fan-shaped propeller or screw in a tube, that sucks water through the tube.

JET Stream of fluid forced out under pressure from a narrow opening or nozzle.

JIB A triangular sail usually at the front of a yacht or sailing ship.

KNOT One nautical mile per hour, equal to 1.15 miles per hour or 1.85 kilometres per hour.

LINEN Hardwearing material often used to make a ship's sails.

LINER A large ship that carries passengers.

LABORATORY Somewhere equipped for scientific experimentation or research.

MAST A tall pole on a ship which may hold up sails, radio aerials, radar dishes or even flags.

PUMP A machine used for raising water or other liquids.

RADAR A system using invisible radio waves, beamed out and reflected back by objects as 'echoes'. These are displayed on a screen to help identify other ships, planes, land, icebergs and similar items.

REFINERY Place where oil is turned into petrol.

RIGGED A ship fitted with sails, and the ropes and chains used to control them.

ROLLCAGE A metal framework within some racing boats that prevents crushing in the event of the boat turning over in a crash.

RUDDER A large, wide, flat part which can be tilted from side to side for steering. Usually situated at the rear or stern of a ship.

SAILS Fabric spread to catch or deflect the wind as a means of propelling a ship or boat.

STEEL Very strong metal.

STERN The rear part of a ship or boat.

SATELLITE NAVIGATION A system which tells you where you are, using satellites in space.

SUBMERSIBLE A boat that can function when under water.

TOPGALLANT The top part of a ship's mast.

WINCHES System that lifts something by winding a line around a reel.

INDEX

Slight water damage 29/9/06